TRAINING
DIG IN

THE DEVOTED WARRIOR

NEXGEN

Building the New Generation of Believers

COOK COMMUNICATIONS MINISTRIES
Colorado Springs, Colorado • Paris, Ontario
KINGSWAY COMMUNICATIONS LTD
Eastbourne, England

NexGen® is an imprint of
Cook Communications Ministries, Colorado Springs, CO 80918
Cook Communications, Paris, Ontario
Kingsway Communications, Eastbourne, England

DIG IN: TRAINING MANUAL
© Copyright 2006 by Ron Luce

All rights reserved. No part of this book may be reproduced without written permission, except for brief quotations in books and critical reviews. For information, write Cook Communications Ministries, 4050 Lee Vance View, Colorado Springs, CO 80918.

First Printing, 2006
Printed in the United States of America
1 2 3 4 5 6 7 8 9 10 Printing/Year 11 10 09 08 07 06

Written by David and Kelli Trujillo
Cover Design: Marks & Whetstone
Interior Design: Helen Harrison

All Scripture quotations, unless otherwise noted, are taken from the HOLY BIBLE, NEW INTERNATIONAL VERSION®. Copyright © 1973, 1978, 1984 by International Bible Society. Used by permission of Zondervan Publishing House. All rights reserved. Scripture quotations marked MSG are taken from *THE MESSAGE*. Copyright © 1993, 1994, 1995, 1996, 2000, 2001, 2002 by Eugene Peterson. Used by permission of NavPress Publishing Group. All rights reserved.

ISBN: 0-78144-435-7

CONSTITUTION CONUNDRUM

YOU'VE JUST BEEN put in charge of a land with one million inhabitants and have been given the job of immediately drawing up a plan for how this nation will be run. What kind of government will you put in place? What will be the laws of the land? Your job is to work together in your team to quickly write a short "constitution" that covers these four issues:

What type of government will you have: a monarchy, a democracy, a communist republic, or some other type of government?

What is the most important law of the land?

What will be the most important rights of citizens in your country?

What will be your policy toward war? Will you have a draft or a volunteer army?

DIG IN

MY LORD AND MY GOD

ONE WAY WE CAN understand the meaning of the word *lord* is to look at how it was used in English in the Middle Ages. Feudal lords were people who owned and oversaw large areas of land. They allowed people called *vassals* to live on the land in order to farm it or do other types of work on it. Though the vassals had homes, it was clear that the property belonged to the lord. In this sense, a lord was the owner of a vassal's home and livelihood.

THE VASSAL WAS obligated to serve the lord by fighting on his side in any military battle; in this way, the lord was the commanding officer of the vassal. The vassal also had to provide food and money for the lord—similar to the way people pay rent today. In this way, the vassal acknowledged the lord's rule over his life. The lord had input into what vassals did for a living and even had the right to arrange marriages for a vassal's children. All vassals had to make a public oath of faithfulness to their lord (called an "oath of fealty").[1]

Talk about these questions together:

How does this usage of the word *lord* give you new insight into what it means to call Jesus your Lord? Explain.

What similarities do you see between Jesus' role as Lord in your life and the relationship between the feudal lords and the vassals in the Middle Ages? What differences are there?

Read Romans 10:9. According to the *Wycliffe Bible Dictionary*, in this Scripture the Greek word translated *lord* means "master, owner, one with power and authority." How is this like or unlike the English meaning of *lord*?

What difference would it make if Romans 10:9 was translated as "Confess with your mouth that Jesus is your *owner*" or "Confess with your mouth that Jesus is your *master*"?

How does this idea of Jesus' "lordship" help you understand what it means to follow Jesus as your King? Be specific.

DIG IN

United States of America

NATURALIZATION OATH

"I hereby declare, on oath, that I absolutely and entirely renounce and abjure all allegiance and fidelity to any foreign prince, potentate, state or sovereignty of whom or which I have heretofore been a subject or citizen; that I will support and defend the Constitution and laws of the United States of America against all enemies, foreign and domestic; that I will bear true faith and allegiance to the same; that I will bear arms on behalf of the United States when required by the law; that I will perform noncombatant service in the Armed Forces of the United States when required by the law; that I will perform work of national importance under civilian direction when required by the law; and that I take this obligation freely without any mental reservation or purpose of evasion; so help me God."[2]

THE BATTLE

Because the Greek text allows for some variation of meaning in this case, several versions of the Bible translate Matthew 11:12 differently. READ MATTHEW 11:12 IN YOUR BIBLE.

How does your Bible's translation compare or contrast with the *English Standard Version* translation: "From the days of John the Baptist until now the kingdom of heaven has suffered violence, and the violent take it by force"?

What insights do these different wordings give you?

What does this passage tell you about the strength and courage required of warriors in God's kingdom?

When might a Christian teenager need to exhibit this kind of strength and courage? Give an example.

What does it mean to you to be a warrior for the King? How does it make you feel to know that God wants to use you in this way?

Pray together as a group, committing to be warriors for your King and asking God to give you the strength and courage you need for the battle.

DIG IN

ONWARD CHRISTIAN SOLDIERS

by Sabine Baring-Gould

ALL:
Onward, Christian soldiers, marching as to war,
With the cross of Jesus going on before!
Christ, the royal Master, leads against the foe;
Forward into battle see his banner go!

GIRLS:
At the sign of triumph Satan's host doth flee;
On then, Christian soldiers, on to victory!

GUYS:
Hell's foundations quiver at the shout of praise;
Brothers, lift your voices, loud your anthems raise!

ALL:
Like a mighty army moves the Church of God;
Brothers, we are treading where the saints have trod.

GIRLS:
We are not divided, all one body we:
One in hope and doctrine, one in charity.

GUYS:
Crowns and thrones may perish, kingdoms rise and wane,
But the Church of Jesus constant will remain.

ALL:
Gates of hell can never against that Church prevail;
We have Christ's own promise, and that cannot fail.

MATCHING MOTTOES

Work together to match each city below with its motto. (Indicate matches by drawing lines from a city to a motto.)[3]

CITIES

Anchorage, Alaska

Atlanta, Georgia

Baltimore, Maryland

Boston, Massachusetts

Chicago, Illinois

Denver, Colorado

Houston, Texas

Indianapolis, Indiana

Las Vegas, Nevada

Los Angeles, California

Miami, Florida

Milwaukee, Wisconsin

Minneapolis, Minnesota

Nashville, Tennessee

Philadelphia, Pennsylvania

Portland, Oregon

Roswell, New Mexico

San Francisco, California

Seattle, Washington

MOTTOES

Gateway to the Americas

The City of Brotherly Love

The Mile High City

The City by the Bay

The City that Reads

The Emerald City

The World's Next Great International City

The Circle City

The Aliens Aren't the Only Reason to Visit!

The Cream City

City of Lakes

Beantown

City of Lights

The Entertainment Capital of the World

The City of Roses

City of the Angels

The Space City

The Music City

The Windy City

DIG IN

OBEDIENCE WITH ALL YOUR HEART

PASS AROUND THE OBJECTS you've been given, and hold them as you talk about what obedience really means. Talk about these questions together.

1. Why do you think some people view obedience to God like a leash or a chain?

2. When has the idea of obeying God felt like a leash to you? Are there areas in your life in which you're straining against God's law (like leashed dogs do when they're trying to run from their owner) instead of willingly obeying?

3. Why do you think God didn't create us like video game characters or robots that He could control 100 percent? Why does He give us the choice to obey or disobey?

4. How is clay a good symbol of obedience? What are other objects or ideas you think could represent what obedience really means?

5. How do you want to grow in obedience? In which area of your life or in what specific situation do you know you need to obey God?

WORK INDIVIDUALLY to form your pieces of clay into a symbol of obedience. You could create a heart, a cross, a person, or any other image you think represents your commitment to obey God. Share your clay objects with your group.

When everyone in your group is done, lay your clay items at the foot of the cross in the front of the room to symbolize your commitment. Then quietly return to your seats.

MY PRAYER

Write a prayer about your desire to grow in devotion and obedience in these areas:

HEART...

MIND...

SOUL...

STRENGTH...

OTHER AREAS OF YOUR LIFE...

Worship Jesus as the authority over the universe . . . and over your **LIFE**.

DIG IN

BEFORE JESUS WAS CRUCIFIED, He was beaten and whipped brutally. His back would have been severely bloodied after the whip tore through skin and muscle. Jesus was then nailed by each wrist to the cross. Then His feet were placed atop each other, and a large nail driven through the arch of each, affixing them to the cross.

DEATH ON A CROSS

Physician C. Truman Davis wrote a medical analysis of crucifixion called "The Crucifixion of Jesus." Here is how he described what Jesus went through next: "As Jesus slowly sagged down with more weight on the nails in the wrists, excruciating, fiery pain shot along the fingers and up the arms to explode in the brain. The nails in the wrists were putting pressure on the median nerve, large nerve trunks which traverse the mid-wrist and hand. As He pushed Himself upward to avoid this stretching torment, He placed His full weight on the nail through His feet. Again there was searing agony as the nail tore through the nerves between the metatarsal bones of His feet. At this point, another phenomenon occurred. As the arms fatigued, great waves of cramps swept over the muscles, knotting them in deep, relentless, throbbing pain. With these cramps came the inability to push Himself upward. Hanging by the arms, the pectoral muscles, the large muscles of the chest, were paralyzed and the intercostal muscles, the small muscles between the ribs, were unable to act. Air could be drawn into the lungs, but could not be exhaled. Jesus fought to raise Himself in order to get even one short breath. Finally, the carbon dioxide level increased in the lungs and in the blood stream, and the cramps partially subsided."[4]

JESUS' HEART AND LUNGS WERE WEAKENED until He eventually died. After His death, He was pierced through with a spear.

Alas! And Did My Savior Bleed

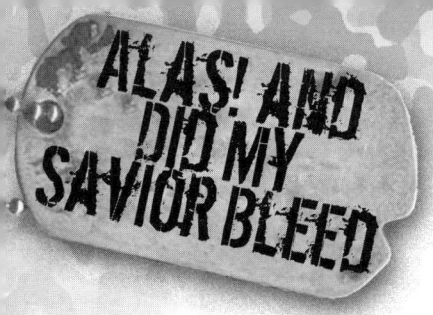

by Isaac Watts

Alas! and did my Savior bleed
And did my sovereign die?
Would he devote that sacred head
For sinners such as I?
Was it for sins that I have done
He suffered on the tree?
Amazing pity! Grace unknown!
And love beyond degree!
But drops of grief can ne'er repay
The debt of love I owe;
Here, Lord, I give my self away—
'Tis all that I can do. Amen.

What is YOUR response to the cross?

THE WORLD'S VALUES VS. JESUS VALUES

BASED ON your own experiences in the world—what TV shows and magazines suggest, what non-Christian friends believe, what the Internet promotes—how would you describe the world's values and mind-set when it comes to these issues? Talk together about each area and come up with some specific examples. Take notes summarizing your main ideas.

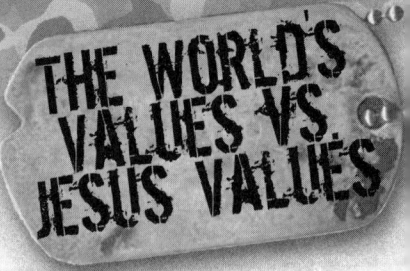

What does the world believe about **MONEY?**

What does the world believe about **FAMILY?**

What does the world believe about **SUCCESS?**

What does the world believe about **SEXUALITY?**

What does the world believe about **FRIENDSHIP?**

What does the world believe about one's **SELF-IMAGE?**

What does the world believe about **THE MEDIA & ENTERTAINMENT?**

NOW CONSIDER what the Bible has to say about these issues. What are God's values? What do you remember from Scripture passages you've read, sermons or teachings you've heard, or books you've read about God's take on these issues? Talk together about God's values for each area and come up with some specific examples. Take notes summarizing your main ideas.

What are God's values when it comes to **MONEY?**

What are God's values when it comes to **FAMILY?**

What are God's values when it comes to **SUCCESS?**

What are God's values when it comes to **SEXUALITY?**

What are God's values when it comes to **FRIENDSHIP?**

What are God's values when it comes to **SELF-IMAGE?**

What are God's values when it comes to **THE MEDIA & ENTERTAINMENT?**

BASED ON YOUR DISCUSSION, what do you think 1 John 2:15 really means?

DIG IN

MY LIFE, MY KING, HIS VALUES...

READ THROUGH THESE QUESTIONS and write down your thoughts. Be brutally honest—this is just between you and God.

RE-READ PHILIPPIANS 4:4-8. Does this describe your life? What influences might Satan be using to keep you from living out these values?

What are some areas in your life in which you've allowed yourself to be influenced by the world?

What is appealing about the world's values in that area? Why do you think you've let your standards slide?

Are you willing to give that up? How could other Christians help you do this?

Take some time to pray, telling God what's on your heart.

DIG IN

MY ACTION STEPS

In your group, read this paraphrase of 1 John 2:15–17 from The Message.

Don't love the world's ways. Don't love the world's goods. Love of the world squeezes out love for the Father. Practically everything that goes on in the world—wanting your own way, wanting everything for yourself, wanting to appear important—has nothing to do with the Father. It just isolates you from him. The world and all its wanting, wanting, wanting is on the way out—but whoever does what God wants is set for eternity. (MSG)

NOW TALK ABOUT these questions:

How does this passage apply to what you just privately thought and prayed about? What words or phrases stand out to you?

How can Christians help each other love God and hate the things of this world? Share some specific ideas with each other.

Has God been speaking to you during this session? If so, how?

Are you willing to share with others one of the areas in your life in which you know you need to renounce the world? If so, go ahead and tell others about it.

Now pray for each other, asking God to help each of you take action on your faith commitments.

DIG IN

LOVE GOD

(hate the world)

(hate God)

LOVE THE WORLD

LOVING THE WORLD?

Read these passages together and take notes summarizing what they say about God's love for the world and how that love is expressed.

JOHN 1:29

JOHN 3:16–17

JOHN 6:33

JOHN 8:12

JOHN 12:46–47

2 CORINTHIANS 5:18–19

1 TIMOTHY 1:15

1 JOHN 4:9–10

DIG IN

TALK ABOUT THESE QUESTIONS:

How would you summarize God's plan of love for the world?

How does the idea of God's love for the world in these passages compare or contrast with our call to "hate" the world? Explain how you think this all fits together.

Why is it important for Christians to understand both meanings of "the world" (the world as the enemy's values and the world as people God loves)?

What happens if a Christian over-emphasizes hatred of the world's values without loving the people of the world?

What happens if a Christian focuses entirely on loving the people of the world without also hating the values of the world?

How can a Christian realistically have balance between hating worldly things and loving the people of the world?

IN THIS WORLD BUT NOT OF IT

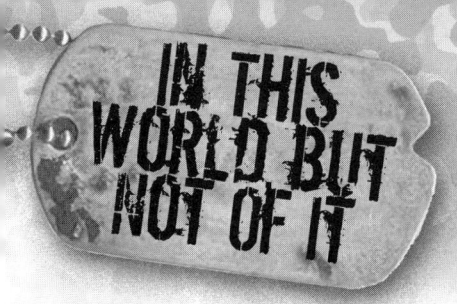

Read these quotes with your partner:

"One must somehow find a way of loving the world without trusting it; somehow one must love the world without being worldly."
— G.K. Chesterton

"This world has nothing for me and this world has everything—all that I could want and nothing that I need."
— "This World," Caedmon's Call

TALK ABOUT THESE QUESTIONS:

What is your response to these quotes? What stands out to you?

Do you relate to these quotes? If so, how?

When have you experienced the tension between being a citizen of God's kingdom while living here on planet Earth?

DIG IN

COURAGE QUANDRIES

Instructions: For each question, circle the answer that you think requires greater courage.

1. Does it take more courage...
...to skydive? **OR** ...to eat worms?

2. Does it take more courage...
...to sing a solo in front of 200 people? **OR** ...to climb a 50-foot ladder?

3. Does it take more courage...
...to apologize? **OR** ...to forgive?

4. Does it take more courage...
...to pray in public? **OR** ...to publicly show kindness to a social outcast?

5. Does it take more courage...
...for someone in a country without freedom of religion to stand up for Jesus even if it means he'll go to prison? **OR** ...for a teenager in America to stand up for Jesus even if it means losing all her friends?

6. Does it take more courage...
...to go up to a stranger and talk to him or her about your faith in Jesus? **OR** ...to talk openly with a good friend (who's not a Christian) about your faith in Jesus?

DIG IN

COURAGE IS:

1. Read these quotes, then circle the one that you think best defines true courage.

"Courage is not simply one of the virtues, but the form of every virtue at the testing point."
—C.S. Lewis[5]

"Courage is almost a contradiction in terms. It means a strong desire to live taking the form of a readiness to die."
—G.K. Chesterton[6]

"Courage is resistance to fear, mastery of fear—not absence of fear. Except a creature be part coward it is not a compliment to say it is brave; it is merely a loose application of the word. Consider the flea!—incomparably the bravest of all the creatures of God, if ignorance of fear were courage." —Mark Twain[7]

"Perfect courage is to do without witnesses what one would be capable of doing with the world looking on."
—Duc de La Rochefoucauld François[8]

"Courage is fear holding on a minute longer."
—General George Patton[9]

"Courage is the art of being the only one who knows you're scared to death." —Harold Wilson[10]

2. Tell your small group which quote you picked and why.

3. Talk together about this question: What other words or phrases would you use to describe courage?

4. Work together in your small group to come up with a definition of courage.

Courage is . . .

_____
_____
_____

DIG IN

WHEN I'VE LET FEAR WIN...

Take some time to write about a specific time recently when you let fear, social pressure, or other things hold you back from living courageously—doing what God wants you to do. Write honestly, because this is just between you and God.

SURRENDERING FEARS EMBRACING COURAGE

READ THESE SCRIPTURE PASSAGES. Reflect on them—what do they mean to you? Pray about them, asking God to speak His truth to your heart.

JOSHUA 1:6-9

PSALM 27:1-3

ROMANS 8:31-39

1 CORINTHIANS 16:13

DIG IN

SUPERFICIAL FAITH

Re-read Matthew 13:1–9, 18–23 in your small group. Then talk about these questions and take notes on your thoughts.

Based on what you've read, how would you define *superficial faith*?

What does superficial faith look like in today's terms?

Now apply the parable in Matthew 13 to everyday life for teenagers. What's a scenario you can think of—real or made up—in which a teenager's response to faith is like the seed snatched up by the birds?

Describe a modern-day situation of a teenager whose faith is like the seed that landed on shallow soil.

Now, describe a modern-day situation of a teenager whose faith is like the seed that grew among thorns.

In addition to what you described in your examples, what are some other factors that can cause teenagers today to have a "shallow" or superficial faith?

DIG IN

DEEP-ROOTED FAITH

TALK ABOUT THESE QUESTIONS TOGETHER:

What is your response to Polycarp's story? What about it stands out most to you?

Which is the more amazing feat—being martyred for his faith or living faithfully for 86 years?

When you think of the course of your own life and imagine yourself in your 80s or 90s, what do you want your faith to be like? Describe it.

What steps do you need to take now to build toward that kind of faith in your old age?

Review the "Faith Fertilizers" in the margin box. Are there additional faith fertilizers that are meaningful to you? How do they help you grow?

In which of these areas do you need to grow in order to have a deep-rooted faith? Commit to God and pray with your partner about developing one area in the immediate future.

FAITH FERTILIZERS

Regular time in the Bible

Regular time in prayer

Christian friendship (encouragement, accountability)

Involvement in corporate worship

NOW take a moment to think through the themes and ideas of the past seven sessions. (Feel free to flip through this Training Manual to remind yourself.) How would you sum up the main spiritual growth steps you want to take now that we've concluded **DIG IN**?

NOTES

NOTES

ENDNOTES

1. Adapted from the factual information found at http://www.britainex press.com/History/Feudalism_and_Medieval_life.htm (accessed October 2005).
2. uscis.gov/graphics/services/natz/oath.htm (accessed October 2005).
3. http://www.usacitiesonline.com/mottosa-b.htm (accessed October 2005).
4. The quote describing Jesus' crucifixion can be found at http://www.our catholicfaith.org/crucifixion.html (accessed October 2005).
5. http://www.bartleby.com/63/46/5146.html (accessed October 2005).
6. http://www.bartleby.com/66/87/12187.html (accessed October 2005).
7. http://www.bartleby.com/66/13/62113.html (accessed October 2005).
8. http://www.bartleby.com/66/67/34667.html (accessed October 2005).
9. http://www.quotationspage.com/quote/34483.html (accessed October 2005).
10. http://www.quotationspage.com/quote/29726.html (accessed October 2005).

GET READY TO BUILD ON YOUR
DIG IN: THE DEVOTED WARRIOR EXPERIENCE!

ISBN: 0-78144-416-0 • Item #: 104915
6 x 9 • Spiralbound • 144 pages

You know that Jesus is the Lord of your life. You've been taught to recognize the enemy and are armed with courage, ready to fight the ultimate battle. But where do you go from here?

Let *Over the Edge: Ultimate Submission* be your battle guide as you combat Satan's lies. Over the course of seven weeks, you'll be challenged to live every day totally sold-out to Jesus, your Master and Commander.

Here's what to expect . . . you will:
>> Get a chance to dive deeper into the issues you looked at during *Dig In: The Devoted Warrior*
>> Have a plan to dig into the Word every day
>> Get specific action steps for living a life marked by devotion, defiance, and courage

Don't let one more day pass—learn to live a life of *Ultimate Submission* to the King!

To order, visit www.cookministries.com, call 1-800-323-7543, or visit your favorite local bookstore.

COOK COMMUNICATIONS MINISTRIES